Labour Day

Jessica Morrison

Weigl

Published by Weigl Educational Publishers Limited
6325 10th Street S.E.
Calgary, Alberta
T2H 2Z9

www.weigl.com

Library and Archives Canada Cataloguing in Publication data available upon request.
Fax 403-233-7769 for the attention of the Publishing Records department.

Morrison, J. A. (Jessica A.), 1984-
Labour Day / Jessica Morrison.

(Canadian celebrations)
Includes index.
Also available in electronic format.
ISBN: 978-1-55388-619-8 (hard cover)
ISBN: 978-1-55388-620-4 (soft cover)

1. Labour Day--Canada--Juvenile literature. I. Title.
II. Series: Canadian celebrations (Calgary, Alta.)

HD7791.M67 2010   j394.2640971   C2009-907298-X

Printed in the United States of America in North Mankato, Minnesota
1 2 3 4 5 6 7 8 9 0 14 13 12 11 10

062010
WEP230610

Editor: Josh Skapin
Design: Terry Paulhus

Weigl acknowledges Getty Images as its primary image supplier for this title.
Library and Archives Canada: pages 15, 17.

We gratefully acknowledge the financial support of the Government of Canada through the Canada Book Fund for our publishing activities.

Contents

What is Labour Day?

Labour Day is a national holiday. It takes place on the first Monday in September. Labour Day is a time to celebrate workers across the country. Most people have the day off work to relax and spend time with family and friends.

Working Together

Labour Day is a chance to enjoy the day without work. In Canada, Labour Day represents **fairness** among workers and people working together. Labour Day is celebrated because Canadian workers took a stand for their beliefs more than 135 years ago.

Long Hours at Work

At one time, Canadians had very long work days. Most people worked at least 12 hours each day. In the late 1800s, workers tried to change this. They wanted shorter work days. Workers in Hamilton, Ontario, started the "Nine-Hour Movement." They wanted to work only 58 hours per week. Soon, a group in Toronto worked for this right as well.

On Strike

The Toronto group asked for nine-hour work days. Their request was refused. On March 25, 1872, the group went on **strike**. This meant that they would not work until their needs were met. Workers were brought in from small towns to do the strikers' jobs.

Worker's March

Sometimes, people hold marches to stand up for what they believe in. In April 1872, 2,000 workers began marching in a parade through Toronto. Two **marching bands** led the way. The group wanted to bring awareness to their cause. More and more people joined the parade as the group marched. The crowd grew to about 10,000 people.

Changing Laws

Prime Minister John A. Macdonald heard about the Toronto group's cause. He knew that all Canadians wanted labour laws changed. Macdonald thought Canadians should have the right to work fewer hours. He began making changes to labour laws.

A Canadian Holiday

Prime Minister John Thompson made Labour Day an official holiday in 1894. Since then, Labour Day has been celebrated on the first Monday of September. Soon, news of Labour Day spread across North America.

Labour Day across North America

In 1882, American labour leader Peter J. McGuire saw a labour celebration in Toronto. He brought the idea to the United States. The first Labour Day event in the United States took place on September 5, 1882. Labour Day events began to take place across the country.

End of Summer

In Canada, Labour Day is often one of the last days of summer vacation before school begins. Many people have barbecues and picnics on Labour Day. They may go camping or hiking before **autumn** weather turns cold.

Football Tradition

In Canada, many people enjoy watching or playing football on Labour Day. The Canadian Football League (CFL) hosts the Labour Day Classic on Labour Day weekend each year. The event has rival CFL teams play against each other.

Glossary

| autumn | fairness |
| marching bands | strike |

Index